STRUTTING IT !

JEANNE BEKER
STRUTTING IT !
THE GRIT BEHIND THE GLAMOUR

FOREWORD BY **COCO ROCHA**

≣ TUNDRA BOOKS

Text copyright © 2011 by Jeanne Beker
Foreword copyright © 2011 by Coco Rocha

MAR   2012

Published in Canada by Tundra Books,
75 Sherbourne Street, Toronto, Ontario M5A 2P9

Published in the United States by Tundra Books of Northern New York,
P.O. Box 1030, Plattsburgh, New York 12901

Library of Congress Control Number: 2010926098

Library and Archives Canada Cataloguing in Publication

Beker, Jeanne
Strutting it : the grit behind the glamour / Jeanne Beker.
ISBN 978-1-77049-224-0

1. Models (Persons) – Juvenile literature. 2. Models (Persons) – Biography – Juvenile literature. I. Title.
HD8039.M77B45 2011   J746.9'2092   C2010-902063-4

17.95

We acknowledge the financial support of the Government of Canada through the Book Publishing Industry Development Program (BPIDP) and that of the Government of Ontario through the Ontario Media Development Corporation's Ontario Book Initiative. We further acknowledge the support of the Canada Council for the Arts and the Ontario Arts Council for our publishing program.

ONTARIO ARTS COUNCIL
CONSEIL DES ARTS DE L'ONTARIO

Information on those in the fashion industry changes frequently.
While every attempt for accuracy has been made, we regret any inadvertent omission or error.

Title page photo: JD Ferguson
Design: Jennifer Lum
Printed in Canada

2 3 4 5 6   16 15 14 13 12 11

*To all those beautiful girls that work so hard
at giving us all those pretty pictures.*

CONTENTS

FOREWORD

A DAY IN THE LIFE OF A MODEL

The girl wakes up at 10:30 a.m. and pulls the shades of her New York penthouse apartment on a glorious view of Central Park. Normally she wouldn't emerge from bed this early, but her agent has left her three messages begging her to come to a shoot. At first the client was offering her $10,000, then $15,000, and now $20,000. The girl enters her massive walk-in closet, throws on a custom Dior dress, and heads downstairs to where her driver and limo await. On set, everyone is patiently waiting for her, as are all the items she insists are on hand at every shoot. Whatever she wants, she gets. She poses for a few pictures and, before lunch, announces that she's done. The room applauds, and off she heads to enjoy the rest of the day, spending her paycheck.

Oh, the life of a model. Or so many would think. . . .

Let me give you the lowdown on an actual model's typical day:

The girl wakes up before the sun has risen in the apartment she shares with a dozen other models. She runs to the gym to work out for an hour so that she can try to fit into the dresses she expects will be a size too small for her. She finds her own way to the studio, in the dark, and upon arriving, is informed that the photographer is running three hours late. Once everyone is on hand, the shoot begins. They're on a deadline so they *keep shooting through lunch and on into the evening. Of course, the girl doesn't dare complain because she knows that, if she does, she can easily be replaced. It's dark again outside as she leaves the studio to head home with her paycheck of $200.*

And this is a good day, because this model is actually a working model.

In contrast to an effortless life of glamour, models work hard. Sometimes it means sitting for ten hours at a casting, only to be turned away. Often it means working without breaks, or sleep. It's a difficult career choice, and many of the hardships are only realized when you're actually in the thick of it. As with anything, though, hard work and patience do pay off. In my career as a model, I've been through it all. I've had times when the pressure and expectations were so difficult, I just wanted to quit. But I've also had some amazing experiences that very few could hope to enjoy. I've had opportunities to travel extensively and meet and work with some amazing people. And, yes, I've certainly experienced a few glamourous moments!

Are you ready to be a model? Jeanne Beker has spent an entire career in and around the fashion industry. I've had the privilege to meet her more than a few times and have always enjoyed talking to her. In this book, she presents many of the skills and qualities you'll need to make it as a model. If you follow her advice, I'm sure you'll be far better prepared to start this new venture than most. Like any career, modeling has its highs and lows, but if you're anticipating and equipped for the hardships, you'll go far.

Coco Rocha

NOTES FROM THE FRONT ROW

What I love most about the fashion world are its people: the brilliant designers, the talented behind-the-scenes teams, the savvy editors, the impassioned photographers, the eccentric fashionistas, and those gorgeous girls that "strut it" down the international runways. And as much as I appreciate the exquisite garments, the excitement of travel, and the intrigue of witnessing the whole creative process, the real magic usually happens for me when that first model steps out onto the catwalk: She sets the tone for the designer's vision and has the power to transport us on untold flights of fantasy. Beyond the clothes she wears, her energy and attitude are what capture the imagination.

If the fashion arena is grand theater — and that's the way I've always seen it — then the models are its leading ladies. Over the past twenty-five years, I've had the joy of not only rubbing shoulders with some of these leading ladies, but also watching them grow and blossom. While some may burst on the scene like a blaze of fire, only to be extinguished after a season or two, others continue to burn brightly for years: inspiring us all, setting new trends, and leaving an indelible mark on our style-conscious psyches.

Models are an integral part of a designer's fantasy, like taking a ride on this Chanel carousel.

When Fashion Television was created in 1985, the world had already fallen in love with a strong assortment of iconic models that had graced designer runways and glossy magazines for decades. But, suddenly, there I was with my TV camera, in photography studios and backstage at fashion shows around the world, capturing models behind the scenes, talking to them about their hopes and dreams, questioning them about the true nature of their work, and witnessing the ardor of their individual journeys.

Over the next two-and-a-half decades, I watched, as a whole generation of models became household names. Their celebrity status rose, fell, and sometimes rose again. Our cameras diligently rolled on the whole era of the supermodel in the early 1990s, when those larger-than-life girls "momentarily" became more important than the designers – and almost as rich. I witnessed various waves of international beauties get discovered and grab the global spotlight: models from Canada, Brazil, and Eastern Europe. And I marveled at how trends would come and go – from the welcome breath of fresh air that exotic models brought to the scene to the enigmatic intrigue of the waifs and the utilitarian use of "cookie-cutter" models – those girls that all looked alike. Most recently, I've reveled in the fact that the hottest models working today are those that are multi-dimensional and that work hard at showing the world they're more than just pretty faces.

My experiences as a judge on *Canada's Next Top Model* for several seasons have given me added insight into the art, craft, and business of modeling and have made me acutely aware of the passion and perfection required from those who yearn to make it as models. Be forewarned: As easy and ultra-glam as posing in front of a lens or prancing down a runway may look, the work and tenacity required to do this job well and become a genuine success is mind-boggling. Not only does modeling demand certain physical qualities, but it also requires particular personality traits. Modeling is not for the faint of heart — or the faint of spirit.

Just where the fashion industry is going is anybody's guess. No one has a crystal ball to predict what will be expected of models in the future. But I do know that there's a whole new generation of aspiring models out there as well as a whole new generation of fashion fans captivated by the allure of the business. And while

it's all very well to be inspired and enthralled, it's important to see all sides of this enchanting prism — including the grit behind the glamour. This book is not only designed to help you decide whether modeling is right for you, but also to show you some of fashion's true colors.

Karl Lagerfeld is the master-mind behind Chanel and a mentor to many models.

TWO

DREAMING THE DREAM

"First looks!" cries a harried show producer, amid the backstage frenzy, as hair and makeup teams put finishing touches on the bevy of international beauties about to strut their stuff down the Paris runway. Tension runs high as each dresser diligently stands by, ready to help with all the speedy outfit changes and tricky accessories. Out front, hundreds of the world's most revered and influential fashion journalists, editors, and retail buyers take their seats. Throngs of photographers and TV crews scramble to capture the glamourous front-row celebrities before securing their places at the end of the long, imposing catwalk. Backstage, a kind of controlled mayhem ensues, as the girls, now dressed to the nines, are herded into the show's running order lineup, preparing to reveal the exquisite creations they're wearing for the very first time. Their looks are tweaked last minute by the designer and the stylist. Stress levels run high. The waiting audience is restless. Suddenly, the houselights go down. The music begins. Lights go up and the first model is cued. She takes a breath and steps out, her intent gaze fixed on the enormous bank of lenses and popping flashes before her. With a confident walk, she feels the music and powerfully strides down the mammoth runway. Every eye in the house is on her, drinking in her astonishing beauty and the way she makes that exquisite garment come alive.

Between the media and the guests at a fashion show, the focus can be daunting.

These days, there's a growing number of girls – and boys – who imagine themselves on international runways or on the covers of glossy magazines, winning the public's hearts and making their bid for fame, fortune, and the fabulous life. It's no wonder: Today's media is filled with countless images of assorted models, selling everything from sophisticated style fantasies to toothpaste. We're living in a glamour-obsessed society, and supermodels like Kate Moss, who makes it all look so effortless and exciting, are as celebrated as movie stars.

Popular reality shows, like *America's* and *Canada's Next Top Model* (and there are versions of these shows in many countries around the world), examine what it takes to be a successful model. To some degree, these shows try to expose the highs and lows of pursuing the profession. But, essentially, this programming is produced for its entertainment value, and the scenarios it portrays can't always be taken literally. For instance, these TV episodes are shot over the course of a finite, rather brief time frame. So a model's real development cannot always be realistically portrayed. Sure, the producers of these shows throw a wide variety of challenges at the contestants, all in an attempt to mirror some of what goes on in the "real world" of modeling. But, at the end of the day, embarking on a full-fledged career in the business requires far more drive and dedication than it does being a mere contestant on a reality show.

The models walk the runway in Valentino's final ready-to-wear show in Rome.

Making the decision to wholeheartedly pursue a career in modeling shouldn't be taken lightly. Despite the irresistible luster of the job, there are many pitfalls that are often unforeseen by those with "stars in their eyes." Few young people are really prepared for the amount of relentless hard work, constant rejection, and intense physical and psychological stamina required for this most enigmatic and demanding profession. Besides possessing the right physical proportions, there are many other things you must have in order to do the job well: You have to be able to think creatively, quickly, and like a professional; you have to be extremely self-disciplined; you have to be patient; you have to take direction well; you have to be able to not take criticism personally; you have to be open-minded; the list goes on.

There's a high price to pay for all those perks that seem inherent to the business. Any model worth her, or his, salt will tell you that while it can absolutely make for a wildly exciting, inspiring, and all-around rewarding job, at times it can be brutal: taking you away from family and friends for prolonged periods, building you up to ultimately let you down, and sometimes working you to the point of sheer exhaustion.

Still, for some young people with a penchant for fashion and international travel, a model's job is most coveted. The range of interesting and creative people you get to meet is dizzying. And if one has been blessed with the right physical attributes, talents, and, above all, the passion and personality it takes, entering the profession could be worth a shot.

For decades, high-fashion modeling has been considered an ultra-glamourous occupation. While big runway fashion shows are a more recent phenomenon – in the early days, collections were shown in intimate settings, like small salons, without all the theatrical fanfare – models first began to really make their marks

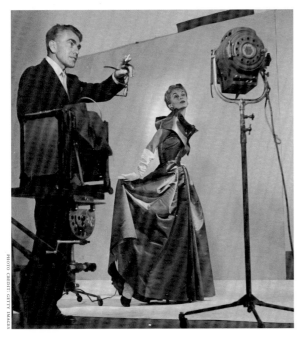

in fashion photography. In the 1940s, legendary photographers Horst P. Horst and Cecil Beaton captured the likes of the elegant Lisa Fonssagrives and the arresting Carmen Dell'Orefice.

Swedish-born Lisa Fonssagrives is considered to be the first supermodel. "I'm just a good clothes hanger," she told Time *magazine in 1949.*

The 1950s saw Suzy Parker become one of Coco Chanel and photographer Richard Avedon's favorite models. Britain's Twiggy rocked the 1960s with her skinny "twiglike" frame, long blonde sweep of a fringe, and signature painted-on lower eyelashes, while the same era also embraced "It girl" Penelope Tree, cool Jean Shrimpton, and ultra-tall "glamazon" Veruschka von Lehndorff. The 1970s celebrated a range of American looks, from the blonde and fair-skinned Cheryl Tiegs and Patti Hansen to the dark-haired,

Legendary model Suzy Parker, advertising executive Kathleen Daly, and famed photographer Richard Avedon on the job in New York, circa 1959.

Model Twiggy revolutionized fashion in the 1960s with her quirky style.

TWIGGY

Birth date: September 19, 1949 (as Lesley Hornby)

Born in: United Kingdom

Agency: Models 1 (London)

Discovered: At the age of 16, by Nigel Davies (later known as Justin de Villeneuve), who helped launch her career

Big break/Career highlights:

- Became the first prominent teenage model
- Known for her large eyes, long eyelashes, and thin build
- Declared the face of 1966 by the UK's *Daily Express*
- Turned to acting and recording
- Models for Marks & Spencer

Career development: Awarded two Golden Globe Awards for her role in *The Boy Friend*; joined the cast of *America's Next Top Model* as a judge; returned to modeling.

Backstage in New York with German-born supermodel Claudia Schiffer, who took the 1990s by storm.

dark-skinned beauty of Beverly Johnson. By the early 1980s, exoticism came more into play with a wider range of models, like the full-lipped Janice Dickinson and the stunning, Somalian-born Iman. In the mid-1980s, vivacious, bigger-boned Cindy Crawford, along with sexy Aussie Elle Macpherson and German bombshell Claudia Schiffer, also ruled the runways, paving the way for those larger-than-life supermodels. Enter the gorgeous Christy Turlington, the incomparable Naomi Campbell, and Canada's own legendary chameleon, Linda Evangelista. The Supermodel Era was in full swing.

By the 1990s, modeling was as much about personality as it was about basic beauty. Superstar Tyra Banks gave it to us in spades, as did quirky girls like Canadian Francophone Eve Salvail, whose shaved, tattooed head gave her an outrageous edge. Canada also presented us with the highly offbeat Jamaican-born Stacey McKenzie and the superb Shalom Harlow, whose prancelike runway walk really set her apart. Fellow American models Amber Valletta and Carolyn Murphy, who would both later make inroads into the acting world, proved that truly great models are certainly not about looks alone. A push was also on for more diversity in modeling: the Sudanese-born Alek Wek and the Malaysian-born Ling, one of the first internationally known Asian models, challenged our ideas of conventional beauty and race.

A host of Brazilian and Eastern European beauties forged into the new millennium, and models like Gisele Bündchen and Karolina Kurkova charmed us with their abilities to strut both haute couture and Victoria's Secret lingerie. But designers began to worry that some of these top girls, who commanded very high fees and perhaps too much attention, were becoming more important than the clothes they were trying to sell. And so, there was an eventual backlash to all these supermodels. And so-called cookie-cutter models – certainly beautiful, but rather generic looking and mostly blonde – began to infiltrate the scene. The feeling from designers was that these fresh young models, capable but perhaps not all that memorable, would show the clothes in a no-nonsense way, never upstaging the creations they sported. After all, the way the designers see it, the clothes should make the fashion world go round – not the models.

But, as we all know, the only constant in fashion is change. Before long, fashion followers craved models that were more interesting. A number of appealing young women, like Canada's Daria Werbowy – who has a very sophisticated look – and the charming and spirited Coco Rocha, started to shine. They appeared on runways and in magazines, along with more exotic models, like America's young Chanel Iman and Britain's Jourdan Dunn. Manchester-born Agyness Deyn also managed to steal the spotlight with her natural, irreverent personal style, and the quirky Romanian-born Irina Lazareanu proved her worth as a muse to famous designers like Chanel's Karl Lagerfeld and Balenciaga's Nicholas Ghesquière. Interestingly, both these girls have not been satisfied with modeling alone and enjoy pursuits in the music field. That could well be the thing that makes them even more intriguing to designers, editors, photographers, and the public.

While people are attracted to modeling for different reasons, one thing they share – whether they admit to being shy or not – is that they adore being in front of a camera lens or on a runway, strutting it for everybody to see. While this business is for those who love being looked at, it often attracts girls that desperately need approval: Perhaps they feel unloved by their parents or never really accepted by their peers. Sometimes, these girls went through an awkward stage growing up because they were too tall or too thin. Maybe they want to use the fashion platform as a way of showing everybody how beautiful they turned out to be. Others might simply think modeling is a good way to see the world and meet stimulating, creative people. And there are those who are just motivated by the money a successful career can bring. But all models have to want to perform and perform at a very intense level. And while their "performances" are on a different scale than those given by stage or film actors, models are bona fide performers nonetheless. They must be prepared to dig deep and exude a range of mood, evoke feelings, project a certain kind of energy, and master the techniques to meet the demands of both the runway and photo shoots. While many models – seasoned or not – are innately insecure, they all have a love of self-expression via fashion. But chances are, they won't go very far unless they consider what unique qualities they can contribute to the industry and pay close attention to image, style, and all that it takes to become a great model.

THREE
GETTING DISCOVERED

I'm constantly surprised by the number of successful models who tell me that they never even considered modeling until they were "discovered" by somebody scouting from an agency. Perhaps it's because, often, those with modeling potential are those who, by the age of fourteen or fifteen, already show signs of having the right physical frame. If an agent comes across a girl who is already fairly tall (most girls have to be, at the very least, 5'8" to do high-fashion modeling), has long, lithe, slender limbs and interesting, well-proportioned facial features, then odds are, that girl will have what it takes, at least physically, for the job.

Agencies are always searching for girls they think will photograph well and for those with an inherent natural beauty. Great cheekbones, clear skin, captivating eyes, and a vibrant smile can make for a compelling face, but not every such face responds well to the camera. Conversely, some girls that may not be all that striking in person manage to turn it on for the camera and look amazing in photographs. Only a trained eye can determine whether or not someone really has the potential to have a shot at success. And the first thing any agent wants to see is how well a girl photographs.

Top modeling agent Elmer Olsen, who's discovered and mentored the careers of countless models who've "made it," says the key to any model's initial success is body shape. "If a girl is 5'11" and has a narrow shape and a long neck, the doors will open to her automatically. It's all in the genes." But Elmer goes on to say that it requires much more than mere physicality to make it. "It takes an easygoing girl – a girl who is relaxed and not too concerned about what people think of her – because she's always going to be going on castings and hearing, 'No, no, no.' She just has to be cool and roll with the punches and have a personality that loves being around people."

We hear lots of suspicious stories of girls being approached out of the blue – on the street, at shopping malls, in restaurants, on the subway, wherever – by strangers that tell them they would make a great model. Then they give the girl their card and ask her to call and come in for some "test-shooting." While those who make

"Transformation": (above) Amanda Laine BEFORE. (right) Amanda Laine AFTER she is glamorized by her agency.

the approach may, indeed, be a legitimate scout from a legitimate agency, most often, they're not: Girls need to be extremely cautious.

There are really only a precious handful of reputable agencies in any big city and very few, if none at all, in small towns. These agencies, and the individuals that claim to represent them, must be checked out with the utmost care by the girl and her parents. All good agencies have sophisticated websites you can visit to find out who they already represent. And, without question, you have to "ask around." Ask to speak with some respected clients of the agency and with a couple of the models the agency claims to represent. If you are under the age of eighteen, get a parent or guardian to make the inquiries. There are lots of shady characters out there that prey on young hopefuls, and they are not to be trusted. And countless aspiring photographers are keen to shoot attractive, young, wannabe models for their own purposes. Unless a photographer is recommended to you by a legitimate and highly reputable modeling agency, beware.

"Transformation": (above) Justine Boomer BEFORE. (right) Justine Boomer AFTER she is glamorized by her agency.

Agencies are always eager to find new faces with potential, and they all have special days, sometimes as often as once a week, where aspiring models can drop by and be seen by the experts. If an agent really believes you have what it takes, he or she will send you to a photographer for test-shooting. Sometimes, the agency might ask you to pay the photographer a minimal fee – it's simply a small investment you may have to make. And it's still no guarantee that this particular agency will sign you or make any sort of commitment. But, at least, you'll have some competent shots to take around to other agencies. However, if the agency is impressed with the test-shoot, you may be on your way to a real relationship with that agency. But always keep in mind that just because one agent says "no" doesn't mean that you aren't right for another. Different agents may be looking for different things – new girls to complement or round out the existing "roster," or stable, of models they already represent. Rejection is commonplace. Anybody who aspires to be part of this business must get used to it, handle it with grace, and move on.

Once they are signed, many girls are miffed when an agent tells them they have to lose a few pounds if they're serious about modeling. This is an extremely sensitive subject because, most of the time, the girls feel they're already trim enough and aren't particularly interested in dieting or even working out. The truth is, no one wants to work with a model who isn't healthy and in top form. The physical demands of modeling are just too great. And no one is interested in promoting "sickly" images of girls any longer. So it's paramount to always eat a balanced diet and make sure you get enough rest and exercise.

Still, some of the strange, harsh, and crazy-making realities of the fashion business are that people can appear up to ten pounds heavier on camera, and the sample sizes that models have to wear are usually a size four or smaller. There's no getting around it: High-fashion modeling takes beauty, height, the right body type, talent, and hard work.

In an upcoming chapter, we'll look at some of the other rewarding types of modeling you can pursue if you're not tall or lean enough for high-fashion work. But, like it or not, designers and editors have a very particular esthetic in mind when they cast girls for their collections, campaigns, or photo spreads, and, usually, that esthetic means having an extremely tall and lean frame. It may all change one day, as concepts of beauty evolve over time. But for the past twenty-five years, that's just the way it is. And that, my dears, is the cold hard truth.

Some people believe that attending a modeling school is the first step to becoming a model. While there *are* some reputable schools out there, most successful high-fashion models have never attended any such school. Various agencies do have in-house "schools" to train some of their younger models, but the vast majority will not care whether a model they wish to represent has or hasn't gone for lessons. Modeling schools are mostly aimed at confidence-building and teaching the best ways of presenting yourself – not the kinds of things you usually have to take formal lessons in. Any agency that requires you to enroll in their school before they sign you is highly questionable. If they strongly believe in your potential, they may even offer to enroll you in their modeling school at little or no cost.

Large-scale competitions have the ability to unearth some spectacular models, and, while winning such a competition is no guarantee that a girl will go on to have an exceptional career, a few local and global competitions have been responsible for launching many aspiring models into the high-fashion stratosphere. For example, for over thirty years now, Ford Models has held an annual competition, in varying cities around the world, called Supermodel of the World. Past winners include Monika Schnarre and Tricia Helfer. Chanel Iman was a first runner-up one year, and Adriana Lima was a contestant. Elite Model Management also holds an international competition, called Elite Model Look, in fifty-five countries. Past notable contestants include Cindy Crawford, Karen Mulder, Gisele Bündchen, and Linda Evangelista.

CINDY CRAWFORD

Birth date: February 20, 1966

Born in: United States

Agency: Elite Model Management (NYC)

Discovered: At the age of 16, by a local photographer, while a student at DeKalb High School

Big break/Career highlights:

- Was a finalist at 17 in the Elite Model Look competition
- Studied chemical engineering as a scholarship student at Northwestern University
- Moved to New York to pursue modeling
- Appeared on over 1000 magazine covers worldwide, including *Vogue*, *Elle*, *W*, *Harper's Bazaar*, *Cosmopolitan*, and *Allure*
- Walked runways for the top designers, including Karl Lagerfeld (for Chanel), Ralph Lauren, and Dolce & Gabbana
- Was featured in countless ad campaigns, including Versace and Calvin Klein
- Became the first modern supermodel to pose for *Playboy* at the height of her career
- Hosted *House of Style* for MTV for six years
- Created, produced, and starred in bestselling exercise videos
- Co-wrote the instructional makeup book *Cindy Crawford's Basic Face*
- Michael Kors said, "Cindy changed the perception of the sexy American girl from the classic blue-eyed blonde to a more sultry brunette with brains, charm, and professionalism."

Career development: Acts; models; is an astute businesswoman with a line of skincare products called Meaningful Beauty, a successful Cindy Crawford Home collection, and a partnership with retail giant JCPenney to promote a home furnishings and accessories line called Cindy Crawford Style; married Richard Gere; currently married to Rande Gerber, with whom she has two children.

For the most part, though, while these competitions can open the door for an aspiring model by helping her get her start, giving her the right representation, the right direction, and good exposure, it's ultimately up to the model herself to live up to everyone's expectations and deliver.

In the 1980s and 90s, Cindy Crawford became one of the world's most adored supermodels.

Another entry platform into the international modeling scene is the Boot Camp that is staged annually by the Elmer Olsen Agency in Toronto. Girls from across Canada are handpicked for this two-day session by agency-owner Elmer Olsen. He finds these hopefuls via open castings, or just walking on the street, and signs them up to be represented by his agency. Then agents from around the world fly in while these girls are put through their paces, demonstrating how much modeling talent and potential they actually have. In the process, the girls learn everything from how to walk a runway to how to apply makeup to how to exercise properly, even in the confines of a small hotel room. This isn't a conventional "competition," but rather a platform for securing global representation. The international agents get a chance to really study a girl's potential, and, if she wins their hearts, they'll sign her. The first year's successful candidate was Tara Gill, and the next year's Boot Camp "winner" was Elise Hélène Gatschene, who ended up walking the Paris runways shortly thereafter.

Former showroom model Karen Lee Grybowski, who also possesses a master's degree in education, heads up the Karen Lee Group in New York. Her company scouts models and mentors those aspiring to be models in workshops, which she holds across the United States. Karen, who's worked with big respected agencies like Wilhelmina and Elite, not only helps develop and place models in the industry, but also advises parents and consults about other opportunities in the fashion world if modeling isn't right for you.

Some of the most popular phenomena of reality TV are *America's* and *Canada's Next Top Model*. These shows pit young hopefuls against one another and, over the course of each "cycle" of the series, put these girls to the test. Each week, one girl is woefully eliminated, until the lone "winner" remains.

Meaghan Waller, who took the title of Canada's Next Top Model, Cycle 3, went from geek to chic.

Among other prizes, the successful contestant gets a hefty modeling contract with the show's main sponsor, automatic representation by a good agency, and the chance to appear in a fashion-magazine editorial spread. On *Canada's Next Top Model*, for example, the big prize was a $100,000 modeling contract with Procter & Gamble.

One of the problems inherent in this type of competition is that applicants must be eighteen years of age or older to enter. In the real modeling world, most of the girls with true superstar potential are already well into the throes of gaining international experience by that age. By the time they're twenty-one or twenty-two, they're full-fledged professionals; some are at the height of their careers. To think of a girl who's already twenty-two just beginning a modeling career is a little unrealistic. But reality television doesn't literally live up to its moniker. As most people who work in the medium will attest, it's all for the sake of entertainment. And even though some of these reality show "winners" do not ever make it in the grand scheme of things, the exercise is a wonderful opportunity to get your foot in the door and gain "show-business" experience. It certainly provides an excellent crash course in modeling, and even though a girl may not come out on top, with all that exposure, she has a decent chance of being signed by an agency and getting at least some commercial work. But, all in all, precious few of the *Next Top Model* winners have gone on to big successful careers.

And just a word of warning about actually "signing" any contractual agreement with an agency: If you're lucky enough to find a reputable agency that's keen to represent you, it would be wise not to get yourself locked into any long-term arrangement. While some agencies would understandably want you to sign an official agreement outlining the terms of representation, make sure that you have an "out" clause – perhaps thirty days. That way, you're free to leave and seek other representation if things don't work out.

When signing any legal agreement, it's of utmost importance to have a parent, guardian, or lawyer advise you. Eager young models can easily be taken advantage of: Keeping your options as open as possible is the best rule of thumb.

FOUR
DEVELOPING YOUR PERSONAL STYLE

"Style" is a word that's thrown around a lot in the fashion world. It's what sets designers apart from one another. It's what gives the writers and editors that cover the scene their unique edge. It's what makes certain photographers right for certain assignments. On a personal level, it's what those of us who love fashion try to develop for ourselves. Style is one of the major things that makes people so intriguing, and it's a powerful tool for communication. The way we dress – the clothes we choose, how we put them together, and ultimately how we wear them – can make a strong statement about who we are as individuals. Bold choices in color or design and mixing clothes in brave or unusual ways usually indicate a strong sense of confidence. Choosing to wear whimsical garments or accessories might tell people that you're playful, with a great sense of fun. Dressing meticulously could give the impression that you have a strong sense of order and take yourself pretty seriously. Dressing sloppily or unimaginatively could be a sign that you're not that inspired by fashion. All these "style" messages could be important when it comes to the impression you're trying to make. And since fashion is a world that often revolves around outward appearances, and since so many in the industry are consumed with "image," the way a model presents *off* the runway can be just as crucial to her career as the way she presents herself *on* the runway.

Certainly, once a model has a decent "book" – a collection of photographs and tear sheets from magazines that show the range she's capable of – her work might speak for itself in terms of getting her "booked" for other jobs. But she will often have to personally go to meet the photographers, designers, editors, or clients that are interested in possibly hiring her. And if she doesn't make a favorable impression in the style department, it could cost her the job. As well, most new models constantly attend "go sees" – big, open, casting calls where dozens of girls vie for the same job. It's imperative to not only make a great impression, but to remain memorable in the eyes of those with the power to employ you.

As a model, you always have to be "on." That's not to say you should go overboard with lots of makeup and elaborate wardrobe choices. Quite the contrary. A minimal amount of makeup is best, so not to mask your natural beauty. And being overdressed looks like you're trying too hard to be noticed.

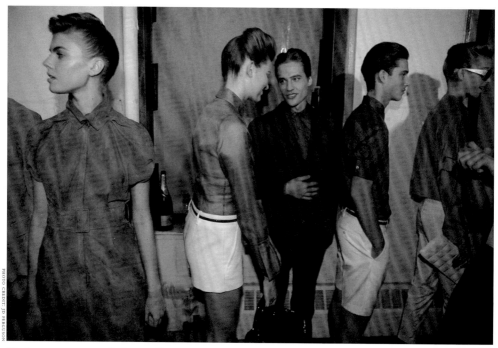

Backstage, moments before walking the runway, everyone is filled with anticipation.

Personal style is something that every model pays more and more attention to the further along she goes in her career. And that makes perfect sense, as she inevitably learns so much from all the designers and stylists she works with. "Being in this world is a like a crash course in style," says Jessica Stam, the successful Canadian model who grew up on a farm in Kincardine, Ontario. "Working with all the top designers is surreal. Now I can tell if a dress is really made well." But until a model begins traveling to the world's fashion capitals regularly and rubbing shoulders with all those fashion-savvy movers and shakers, it's really her own responsibility to learn as much about style as possible. She needs to discover what approach to dressing plays up her best physical assets and communicates what she really wants to say about herself.

It never ceases to amaze me that so many of the aspiring models I've met on *Canada's Next Top Model* know so little about fashion in general. I just assume that any girl who's so determined to make it as a model is not only innately interested in the fashion world, but passionate about it. She should be up on her designers and the collections they create as well as be familiar with the style of the major fashion photographers she may one day be fortunate enough to work with. Unless the aspiring model is living under a rock, there's a wealth of information out there

– in magazines, newspapers, on television and the Internet. I'm never impressed by those who tell me they desperately want to model, but are unable to rhyme off at least a few international designer names, let alone pronounce them right.

Catching up with the bohemian and artsy Irina Lazareanu at the Chanel show in London.

With all this information and so many options available, honing in on what's right for you style-wise can be daunting. But the more you're exposed to, the more you'll formulate your own opinions about what you like and what you don't. Try different looks and experiment with various approaches to fashion. After all, they can be some of the most exciting aspects of becoming involved. But while most of the garments that a model eventually wears "on the job" are from high-end designer collections, her personal wardrobe doesn't have to include any designer labels at all. These days, all kinds of wonderful, fun, trendy, and fashion-forward garments are available at affordable prices: You just have to be a smart shopper.

Vintage clothing and accessories also have great style appeal and are highly appreciated by just about everybody who works in fashion. Even though actual designer vintage clothing and accessories can be pricey, many thrift shops offer gently used pieces that are often more interesting than what's currently available and make for great conversation pieces. By scouring vintage and thrift stores and examining the designs of the past, you will have a better understanding of fashion in general. So many present-day designers look to the past for inspiration and sometimes just revamp existing styles. Remember, anyone with money can go into a fancy designer boutique and buy a hot new bag or a fabulous pair of shoes. But the people you will eventually encounter in the fashion world – editors and designers included – will be much more impressed by you if they see some attempt at creativity. People are always charmed by the unexpected, and in fashion, originality rules supreme.

Many years ago, I covered one of Kate Moss's early photo shoots. I'd never met her before and was intrigued by her irreverent personal style, which included old running shoes, a kind of "shrunken" sweater that looked as though it came from a thrift shop, and a little vintage neckerchief: a far cry from the luxurious labels that she's so famous for sporting today. But, even then, I could tell that this young model, who would one day rule the world's runways, had an innate

KATE MOSS

Birth date: January 16, 1974

Born in: United Kingdom

Agency: Storm Model Management (London), IMG Models (NYC), D'management Group (Milan), and Marilyn Agency (Paris)

Discovered: At the age of 14, at JFK International Airport, by the owner of Storm Model Management

Big break/Career highlights:

· Hired for the Calvin Klein Jeans advertising campaign in 1993

· Inspired the waif period

· Had extremely influential personal style

· Inspired exhibits and modern pieces of art (by Lucian Freud and Chuck Close)

Controversy: Caught doing cocaine by the British tabloids. After the headlines, she was dropped by several labels and campaigns.

Career development: Launched a clothing line for British retailer Topshop; launched a perfume line; mothered a child with magazine editor Jefferson Hack.

With the help of some high-profile campaigns, the sensational Kate Moss is one of the most memorable models of our time.

sense of style. She'd put these pieces together in a seemingly casual manner that looked refreshingly easy. Yet you could tell that she'd carefully considered each piece before she put it on. Above and beyond the way she was dressed, though, was something very endearing: Kate had a sense of humility about her. She was totally cool and cooperative with her creative team, even though some of the clothes on set did not fit her properly. We'll examine that professional attitude that models must have in an upcoming chapter, but I wanted to mention it now because it really does reflect a kind of personal style. Remember, style isn't just about the clothes we wear: It's also about the way we choose to move through the world.

Many models throughout modern history have used their unique personal style to set them apart from the pack and help make a name for themselves. Twiggy had her funky hairstyle, signature lashes, and painted-on freckles. Peggy Moffitt, another popular 1960s model, had her jet black hair cut in an edgy geometric style and her eye makeup very dark and heavy. Of course, showing up to a casting call or "go see" with such an extreme look could turn some potential clients off. And, today, some agents may even dissuade their girls from adopting a particular look. But Peggy Moffitt's dynamic personal style bespoke her strong artistic sensibility, and many photographers were eager to work with her.

Piercings and tattoos have been known to get some models varying degrees of attention. Quebec's Eve Salvail certainly turned heads in the late 1980s with the tattoos she sported on her shaved scalp. And Sybil Buck, the red-haired American model who came into prominence in the early 1990s, was celebrated for the bold nose ring she always wore. Although unique tattoos and piercings can give a girl a distinct identity, they can also get in the way of a designer's vision. Sometimes they actually cost a girl a job. While most of the girls I see backstage at the international fashion shows do sport some sort of discreet tattoo, I would dissuade any girl from going too far with these permanent body decorations. A classic designer evening gown can look odd on a girl with a big, visible, hard-core tattoo, and the designer might not appreciate the body art. On the other hand, some designers don't seem to mind tattoos at all. And when it comes to photo shoots, tattoos can often be "Photoshopped" out of the picture.

An easier and more practical way to "shock" people and get tongues wagging is changing your hair – the style or color or both. While agents may encourage their girls to keep their hair long, a lot of models that bravely cut their hair into interesting new styles are subsequently responsible for launching trends. Legendary Canadian supermodel Linda Evangelista, who quickly became known as a human chameleon, garnered new interest each time she changed the color of her hair, injecting new life into her already successful career. More recently,

Manchester's Agyness Deyn delighted fashion fans with her bold ultra-short crop, bleached platinum blonde. Coupled with her eclectic approach to dressing, largely comprised of striking vintage pieces, and her winning personality, Agyness has garnered a reputation as one of the world's most stylish models.

Manchester-born Agyness Deyn is known for her extraordinary sense of style and offbeat personality.

AGYNESS DEYN

Birth date: February 16, 1983 (as Laura Hollins)
Born in: United Kingdom
Agency: Models 1 (London), Women Model Management (NYC), Why Not Model Management (Milan), and Viva Models (Paris)

Discovered: Shopping on the streets of London, while at college studying drama and music

Big break/Career highlights:

- First signed to Select Model Management
- Caught the attention of casting agents with her short hair
- Known for her unique and changing hairstyles
- Featured on the covers of British *Vogue*, *Time* magazine's Style & Design issue, Italian *Vogue*, and *POP* magazine
- Became the face of Anna Sui, Burberry, Giorgio Armani, Mulberry, Paul Smith, and more
- Was guest editor of *ID* magazine in May 2008, which was dedicated to her
- Was ongoing supporter of childhood friend Henry Holland's label, House of Holland
- Applauded for her distinctive style and outgoing persona
- Provided vocals for the single "who" by Five O'Clock Heroes

Career development: Performed in a band called Gene Jacket; designed jewelry with Henry Holland.

But no matter what your personal style, as a model you're expected to give yourself over to the creative team you're working with. And sometimes, they'll want to chop off your beloved locks. Of course, your agent will let you know if this is worth allowing them to do. If it is, generally speaking, you'll have to comply. Get used to it: No matter what you think you look like or how you want yourself portrayed to the rest of the world, the creative team hired to transform you has a particular vision in mind. You must allow yourself to be molded into the fantasy they want to convey, at least for the time they have you booked. And if they do something "semipermanent" to you, like lop off your locks, you're just going to have to live with it temporarily.

FIVE
TECHNIQUE, TALENT, AND "JE NE SAIS QUOI"

What makes a model attractive, appealing, compelling, and unforgettable? Well, there's the obvious physical beauty she possesses, the grace in which she moves, her ability to transform her look, and her dramatic attitude in both photographs and on a runway. Though some of these qualities come naturally, many take time to cultivate. And since the "art" of modeling isn't something that can be formally taught, experience is key when it comes to things like your best angles or which poses look good on a runway.

Experience is also crucial when it comes to establishing your "walk." As the old adage goes, practice makes perfect. Of course, there are professional runway "coaches," like the inimitable "Miss Jay" Alexander of *America's Next Top Model* fame, or the edgy Stacey McKenzie of Walk This Way Workshops — actual seminars that

Stacey McKenzie continues to turn heads with her unusual look and savvy way of strutting.

models can sign up for that offer expert instruction on what does and doesn't work on a catwalk. But it's ultimately up to the model herself to practice her walk and develop a style for herself that's smooth and confident, while doing justice to the clothes that she's wearing.

Let's not forget that a model's job is primarily to sell: Sometimes, she's selling a mere fantasy; other times, a brand in general. Most often, it's a product. And that product is usually comprised of a designer's wares. At the end of the day, the designer is most concerned with showing off his or her clothes. Knowing how to "work a dress" – make it really come alive – is an important skill in a model's repertoire. And she has to work on it.

Since formal modeling schools are sometimes suspect, it's a model's responsibility to school herself in the art and craft of modeling. She has to be a bit of a sponge, watching and listening carefully, and absorb as much as possible from the industry professionals she has the opportunity to work with. Before her career even takes off, she should watch as many fashion shows as possible, study photographs and editorial spreads in magazines, and "play" in front of the mirror – trying to master a wide range of looks and discovering her best angles. She'll also have to hone her walk, which can end up being her most distinctive "signature" – the thing she becomes recognized for. Shalom Harlow, who studied jazz, ballet, and tap as a child, was adored on the runway for her proud prance. Black British model Jourdan Dunn, who wows everyone with how she uses her extraordinary legs, claims she practices her walk diligently in ultra-high heels.

Still, beyond all the inherent talent and technical skill required to succeed, there's one other mysterious ingredient a model needs to be in a league of her own and catapult to star status. "It comes from the inside," says photographer Mike Ruiz, a judge on *Canada's Next Top Model*. It has to do with a girl's sense of herself when she "turns it on" for the cameras or on the catwalk. With some models, it manifests itself as an elegance, as we've witnessed through the work of Linda

Evangelista and Daria Werbowy. With other models, like German bombshell Claudia Schiffer and the inimitable Gisele Bündchen, it's a sensuality. Then there are those who project a sensitive vulnerability, like Russian-born Natalia Vodianova. Models that have a highly unique look, like Yasmin Warsame, Chanel Iman, or Jourdan Dunn, exude an irresistible exoticism.

Backstage at Valentino with Russian super-model Natalia Vodianova, well-known for her philanthropic work.

CHANEL IMAN

Birth date: November 30, 1989

Born in: United States

Agency: Supreme Management (NYC), Elite Model Management (Paris), Visage (Zurich), D'management Group (Milan), and Unique Denmark (Copenhagen)

Discovered: At the age of 17, when she traveled to New York and won third place in Ford's Supermodel of the World contest, although she had been modeling since the age of 12

Big break/Career highlights:

· Won third place at the 2006 Ford Supermodel of the World contest

· Half African-American, half Korean, was named after icons Coco Chanel and the model Iman

· Walked for Custo Barcelona and DKNY in her first runway season, Fall 2006

· Appeared on the cover of American *Vogue* in May 2007

· Appeared in advertising campaigns for Bottega Veneta, Gap, Victoria's Secret Pink, and United Colors of Benetton

· Appeared as a correspondent for MTV's revival of *House of Style*

Career development: Modeling; TV work.

Chanel Iman's sophisticated poise belies her years.

For other models, it's all about their eyes. Red-haired British model Lily Cole – initially known as "the schoolgirl model" since she started her high-fashion career at fourteen and, despite her success, was very serious about pursuing her education – has enormous, hauntingly innocent eyes, giving her an appealing air of vulnerability. Irina Lazareanu's sense of mystery and playfulness give her an unusual edge, while Agyness Deyn's distinctive style and vibrancy make her enormously attractive and memorable. The legendary Christy Turlington is a striking beauty, but her intelligence gives her a definite advantage. Tyra Banks, who went on to develop a hugely successful career as a TV producer and host, always projects a lively personality, while Naomi Campbell exudes inner strength and confidence. Coupled with her flawless beauty, exoticism, and good genes, Naomi's modeling career is experiencing exceptional longevity. Surprisingly, I have always found Naomi to be a little shy. But she, along with all the models that have managed to make indelible impressions on our hearts and minds, is a brilliant performer. Models like Naomi adopt personae for their professional

COCO ROCHA

Birth date: September 10, 1988
Born in: Canada
Agency: Elite Model Management (NYC), Storm Model Management (London), Marilyn Agency (Paris), and Why Not Model Management (Milan)
Discovered: At the age of 14, at an Irish step-dancing competition
Big break/Career highlights:
· Modeled for Anna Sui and Marc Jacobs in her first runway season
· Became a muse to many designers because of her rich and cheerful character
· Met Steven Meisel in February 2006, who wanted her for an editorial
· Danced an Irish jig during the Scottish Highlands-inspired Jean Paul Gaultier show for Fall 2007
· Appeared on the covers of *Vogue*, *W*, Italian *Vogue*, *Harper's Bazaar*, and
  Time magazine's Style & Design issue
· Was the face of advertising campaigns for Balenciaga, Chanel, Dior, D&G, Lanvin, and more
Career development: Tried her hand at covering New York Fashion Week for E! and blogging.

lives and have the uncanny ability to morph those personae into myriad characters – whatever the situation demands. This ability is innate: It can be worked
on but not entirely cultivated, because it's God-given. And it really does lie at
the heart of every great model we've seen.

In recent years, there's been something else that's helped give models, like all
celebrities, an added cachet – the amount of social conscience they demonstrate.
It's not to say that celebrated models have to take up a charitable cause just to
gain attention or satisfy the media. But all well-rounded young women owe it
to themselves to become aware of the world at large and develop a sense of
caring and compassion for those less fortunate. It's very easy to become a victim
of self-absorption, especially in a career like modeling, when so much attention
is focused on you. To put things into perspective and to use their celebrity status
for the good of society, many models dedicate time and energy to a variety of
causes in order to give back and try and make the world a better place. These
girls win a lot of respect for their efforts and, in turn, become so much more
than talented, pretty faces.

Examples include Natalia Vodianova, whose Naked
Heart Foundation helps children in her native Russia
by building playgrounds; Canada's Jessica Stam,
whose work for Charity: Water helps impoverished
villages in developing nations get clean drinking
water; American model Maggie Rizer, who has
become a strong activist for AIDS because her
father died of it; and Canadian top model Coco
Rocha, who has worked selflessly for everything
from environmental causes to helping kids with

*Down-to-earth and widly talented, Coco Rocha brings big
personality to the international runways.*

cancer to speaking out about eating disorders. "I think a lot of girls don't realize that we have a lot of things we can reach out for," says Coco.

Being socially conscious may seem very much "in fashion" these days, but this is the one meaningful trend we all hope is here to stay. More and more, models are proving that they're determined to lead inspiring lives and touch people in ways that go beyond the projection of physical beauty.

At New York's Fashion Week, with the late, legendary makeup artist Kevyn Aucoin and British model Karen Elson.

IT'S TEAMWORK!

On the surface, it appears that models are the stars of the show – the ones who grab the focus and ultimately get to tell the fashion story. They do this with their walk, their poses, and their physical presence. But, in reality, a model's glamourous image is the end result of a great deal of teamwork by seasoned professionals in a variety of jobs. While the model is a vital part of that team, she is only a cog in the wheel of the creative process. The professionals working with her on any given day – for example, the stylist, the makeup artist, the hairstylist, the photographer – can literally make or break her. They are all integral when it comes to making her look good.

Any girl who thinks the world revolves around just her and who develops an egomaniacal, divalike attitude will quickly learn that there's not much room for her in the industry. People abhor working with difficult, self-centered subjects, and if there isn't mutual respect among all members of the team, the end result usually suffers. And remember, as special as a model may be, anyone can be replaced.

In fashion, as in most businesses, relationships are instrumental in making things happen. A strong work ethic, coupled with a pleasant personal demeanor, goes a

Makeup wiz Pat McGrath, who helps create the looks for the world's top designers, is always focused on perfection.

long way. It is essential in not only establishing a model's career, but in making sure her career develops and advances.

Getting ahead and achieving success all start with the relationship a model has with the people who work at the agency representing her. The agent and the model are business partners – one cannot work without the other – and their relationship is built on mutual trust, honesty, and respect. Once the agent agrees to represent the model, that agent will be responsible for helping to develop her career. The agency will send the model to "go-sees," where she'll meet a variety of casting and art directors, photographers, and editors, and sometimes even designers, that are looking for just the right girls with just the right walk to sport their collections on the runway. Besides looking at what a model physically has to offer and reviewing all the pictures in her book, they will also assess her personal style and attitude to determine whether or not they want to work with her. Most of the time, though, these big decisions about who gets hired happen quickly, and choices are often made on the basis of whether or not the model has the right look.

Britain's Lily Donaldson manages to pull off 1940s high glam, even in a bathrobe and hair clips!

A model must learn not to take things personally: Just because she's not right for certain editorial shoots, shows, or campaigns is not to say that she doesn't have a great look or isn't good at what she does. Handling rejection gracefully is one of the toughest parts about being a model, but it becomes a regular, mandatory exercise in every model's career. Those who don't handle rejection well will never make it as models. Being overly sensitive is an extreme handicap in this business and one that must be overcome.

Once a model lands that coveted job, her booker will be her contact, sorting out her schedule and making sure she gets all the details. While the expression "fashionably late" is a popular one and often excuses some dawdlers from arriving on time, in the fashion world, time is money. And a model who's late for her "call time" can end up costing the production a lot of it. Being late also gives those expecting you a poor impression of how seriously you take the job. There will normally be a substantial number of professionals depending on your arrival before they can start their work, from the hair and makeup team to the stylist to the photographer. Showing a lack of respect for them by turning up late will not get things off to a good start.

While the creative ideas of a model are usually appreciated, she has to under-stand that a vision is rather firmly in place before she even gets to the set. She has to be malleable and allow herself to be transformed to the dictates of the creative professionals working with her. The bottom line is, the model should simply go with the flow. If there are any problems – such as the hairstylist wanting to lop off her long tresses when the model knows she's been booked for a shampoo ad the next day – she may have to call her agent or booker for intervention. But, for the most part, major changes to a model's look will have been discussed with her agent prior to the girl's booking.

It's usually recommended that a model leave her ego at the door and put herself in the hands of the pros that are working with her. She may not like how the hairdresser has done her hair, nor approve of the way the stylist has chosen to dress her. And sometimes, the clothes that she has to wear don't fit her properly

The business of beauty is always a huge team effort.

HEIDI KLUM

Birth date: June 1, 1973

Born in: Germany

Agency: IMG Models (NYC)

Discovered: At the age of 18, when she won a national modeling contest called "Model 92" out of 25,000 contestants

Big break/ Career highlights:

- Accepted a modeling contract a few months after graduating from school
- Became famous after appearing on the cover of the *Sports Illustrated* Swimsuit Issue and from her work with Victoria's Secret
- Became a face for high-fashion labels as well as a spokesmodel for companies such as McDonald's, Braun, and Volkswagen
- Was the host, judge, and executive producer of *Project Runway*, for which she received an Emmy Award nomination for each of the first four seasons
- Appeared in both television and film, including *Sex and the City*, *How I Met Your Mother*, *Blow Dry*, and *The Devil Wears Prada*
- Designed shoes for Birkenstock, jewelry for Mouawad, a clothing line for Jordache, and swimsuits. Her two fragrances are called Heidi Klum and Me.

Career development: Acted; became a television host and producer, a businesswoman, fashion designer, artist, and occasional singer. She is married to Musician Seal.

and have to be pinned in awkward ways. But this is where the model must objectify herself: It's as though she's a doll, being dressed up for the pleasure of the professional team at hand. And even though she may not personally approve of how they have her looking, she's got to work that look the best she can and bring the team's vision to life. That's where her creative talent and imagination come into play. And the best models always manage to transcend any prejudices they may have, maintain a positive attitude, and morph into the fantasy that is best for the team. "I'm always so grateful for the teams I get to work with," says Alek Wek, "for giving me that outlet to express myself as a model. I really grow during these creative times."

New York hairstylist extraordinaire Orlando Pita collaborates with some of the greatest designers in the world and, in the process, helps set trends.

"You have to have a lot of patience to be a really great model," says Orlando Pita, one of the world's most creative and in-demand hairstylists. Watching Orlando and his team painstakingly work on models backstage, you can see that patience is golden in the world of modeling. You may have to spend hours in the makeup chair, or sit around backstage waiting while every little detail is attended to, before you do your thing.

Once you're before the camera, there could be a whole set of difficult conditions to contend with: You could be doing a swimsuit shoot in the freezing cold or modeling winter coats in the sweltering heat; your aching feet might be squeezed into shoes that are at least a size too small; your outrageous hairstyle or heavy makeup might feel uncomfortable; the poses you're asked to hold might be difficult or even painful; you could be dead tired, having just gotten off an overnight transatlantic flight . . . the list goes on. But a model must be stoic: No one wants to hear complaints. You'll have to force yourself to rise above it all and focus on the task at hand. The true test of your talent will be to look as though everything is right with the world, even when it's not.

(above) Male models can have lucrative careers, although the stakes aren't usually as high.

Creating fantasy is a team effort in ways that the average person might never realize. Efforts go into the final product even after the model leaves the shoot. Professionals retouch photographs and doctor them with Photoshop in extraordinary ways. As a magazine editor, I, along with my art director, sometimes asked for certain "body parts" to be altered in photographs to make them more appealing. For the purpose of esthetics, we'd even use the head from one shot on the body from another! And to think some people take these fashion-magazine images so literally, they actually aspire to look like the models! An impossibility, to say the least. The world of high fashion is largely about creating illusions.

(left) The physical requirements for male models can be just as difficult to meet as for their female counterparts.

41

REALITY OF THE ROAD

As much as we might imagine a model's life to be the ultimate in glamourous adventures – traveling to the world's fashion capitals; getting to wear the most beautiful clothes on the planet; constantly being photographed by the best photographers in the business; being invited to all the exclusive parties; and rubbing shoulders with famous and fascinating people – there's usually a big fly in the ointment: A model's life can be painfully lonely. Successful international models are never in one place for too long, and young models that are just starting to build their careers often have to spend long stretches – weeks and sometimes months – in faraway foreign places, gaining experience and building their "books." For a girl who is deeply attached to her family and friends, constant travel – especially when a she is only sixteen or seventeen – is both exhausting and emotionally taxing.

There's just no way around it: If you want to earn top dollars, make an indelible mark on the fashion industry, and have the world fall in love with your image, you must pay a big price. Beyond hard work, you have to be willing to pack your bags – sometimes at a moment's notice; say good-bye to family and loved ones; and hop on countless airplanes to far-flung destinations. Of course, if you're

Model Kate Somers and her mother, Gillian, claim that life on the road has made them closer.

under eighteen, reputable agents will ensure that you have a "chaperone" traveling with you. You may be fortunate enough to have a parent or an older relative accompany you on jaunts to New York or Paris or Milan, should you be modeling at the Fashion Week collections. Canadian models Kate Somers and Amanda Laine have often traveled with their parents, and Kate says traveling with her mother is like bringing a friend along. "But it's not just a friend who I enjoy spending time with, but one who's always there during stressful or overwhelming moments – which tend to occur often while balancing school and work!" reflects Kate. Her mom, Gillian, says traveling with her model daughter has been a positive experience for both of them. "Our ability to travel together has done nothing but strengthen the bond between us," she explains. "Kate and I both feel that this has been a wonderful opportunity – we've grown individually, traveled and lived in different cultures, reveled in the energy and creativity of the wonderful people in this business, and made many friends along the way." Most often, though, going on the road means traveling with a representative from your modeling agency. This person will make sure you abide by curfews, get to your bookings on time, and perhaps most importantly, get the proper food and rest you need.

When a model is first starting out and finds herself so many miles from home, her agency will often put her up in a models' apartment or flat, which a group of up-and-coming girls will share. Sometimes, if the girls are especially young, there'll be a "house mother" there to supervise. Instantly, the young model will have a brand-new set of roommates to adjust to – some that will be complete strangers, from different parts of the world. While the odds of having a room to herself are rare, it can often be a wonderful experience getting to know these girls from other cultures. Sometimes, girls that share an apartment or flat become friends for life. But other times, egos collide, and those not willing to live in harmony with their flatmates can have a tough time.

Missouri-native Karlie Kloss charms editors and designers alike with her easygoing sophistication.

It can also be tough to "come home" each evening, after a trying day of work or rejections, and not have your parents or sister or best friend there to console you. Of course, cellphones and computers can be lifelines, but few things can replace someone to talk to face-to-face or the comfort of a good old-fashioned hug.

"The hardest thing for me is just being away from my family so much," laments Karlie Kloss. Although Karlie – who got discovered at thirteen and had a full-fledged modeling career by sixteen – did spend her first seasons with various members of her family in tow (including her three sisters), it's daunting to be away from the family unit. And while hopping on and off airplanes sounds like the height of glamour to some, especially those eager to see the world, not having a friend along can be trying.

"It's isolating traveling by yourself," Jessica Stam confides. "Now how I deal with it is staying connected with my BlackBerry. But it is really, really tough." Like all models with successful international careers, Jessica spends a lot of time on planes. "It's certainly not all glitz and glamour," she stresses. Daria Werbowy concurs, maintaining that the single most difficult thing for her is the actual flying. "I know it's a luxury to fly around the world, but flying by yourself is tough," says Daria.

Girls just want to have fun: Lifelong relationships can develop on the road, with various fashion players becoming part of your extended family.

An international modeling career exposes you to a world of intriguing people, some rather powerful and some who just pretend to be. There are constant temptations to party, and with that kind of socializing often comes the lure of drugs and alcohol, which is ever present. While a model has the right to let her hair down every once in a while, she owes it to herself and her agency to act professionally and not succumb to temptation. The dark side of the business includes some pretty shady characters that could easily take advantage of a naïve young girl without many "big city" experiences, or who is painfully lonely and needs attention any way she can get it. A model must always remember how detrimental irresponsible behavior can be, not only to her career but also to herself as a person. Those who are weak, lazy, and immature will never succeed for long.

Veteran model Angela Lindvall, who balances her high-profile modeling assignments with an earthy, laid-back lifestyle in California's Topanga Canyon, admits that, at the beginning of her career, she had a difficult time fitting in to that

lofty fashion scene. "It was especially hard accepting being in a world that was so different. I was never a fashionista personality," she notes. "I worked very hard to stay humble and stay connected to my roots. You can easily get stuck in the 'bubble' that's this particular world. You always have to remember that there's so much more to life than this!"

Besides keeping your head and heart in check, having a successful career as a model is like running

Backstage at Alexander Wang, with American model Angela Lindvall.

a business: You have to be on your toes at all times and act as though the world is watching because, eventually, if you become truly successful, it really will be.

The public's penchant for celebrities is at an all-time high. And the media has become monstrous in its relentless coverage of the so-called "glamourous scene." Many of the world's top models find themselves at the center of the fuss and attention, relentlessly scrutinized, talked about, and photographed, sometimes in unfortunate situations. It's like that old saying "Be careful what you wish for." So many aspiring models dream of being famous. But with fame comes a whole set of pressures and unwanted attention. And with cameras everywhere – even in cellphones – and pictures being transmitted instantaneously around the world, it's important not be caught in any compromising situation that could harm your image.

NAOMI CAMPBELL

Birth date: May 22, 1970

Born in: United Kingdom

Agency: IMG Models (NYC), Storm Model Management (London), Marilyn Agency (Paris), and D'management Group (Milan)

Discovered: At the age of 15, window-shopping in Covent Garden while still a student at the Italia Conti Academy, by Beth Boldt, a former Ford model

Big break/Career highlights:

- Began as a catwalk model before being hired for high-profile advertising campaigns
- Her first cover was *Elle*, after another model canceled
- Was the first black model to appear on the covers of French *Vogue* and British *Vogue* (Yves Saint Laurent threatened to withdraw all advertising if *Vogue* refused to place Campbell on its cover)
- Became a supermodel of the 1990s
- Has appeared on over one hundred magazine covers

Controversy: Her temper has led to charges laid against her for hitting her assistant and housekeeper with her BlackBerry.

Career development: Wrote a novel, *Swan*; acted and recorded; worked on her charity, Fashion for Relief.

In 2005, supermodel Kate Moss was featured on the front page of London's *Daily Mirror*, doing drugs. Immediately, she lost her campaign with Burberry and Rimmel Cosmetics. Fortunately, she was so loved and respected and such an amazing model that she did manage to bounce back professionally. But it was a close call.

Understandably, many girls can't tolerate the constant invasion of their privacy. Like most people in the public eye, models need to cultivate a bit of a thick skin and not take idle talk and rumors to heart. It's important to be philosophical and try to turn negative experiences into positive ones. The legendary Naomi Campbell, who's had more than her share of scandals to deal with in the media, once told me that she believes all these "bad experiences" happen for a reason. "You have to take that signal and say, 'What am I supposed to learn from this?'" she advises. "I think my attitude is to just laugh and keep going with what I'm doing. I can't pay much attention to it."

EIGHT

MUSES, SPECIALTY MODELS, AND HARDWORKING GIRLS

While there are many little girls who fantasize about capturing the international fashion spotlight, only a precious few grow up to become "stars." Even if they're lucky enough to get discovered and sign with an agency, their chances of becoming a supermodel are tantamount to winning a lottery. However, if an aspiring model can't manage to have a big international career, there are other avenues she can explore in modeling that might satisfy her and prove financially rewarding at that.

Most working models never do become household names. But they still can cultivate lucrative, fulfilling careers, travel the world, meet interesting people, and let their creative juices flow on runways and editorial shoots. They may not have internationally recognizable faces or ever get signed to any big contracts, but they do get to strut it with the best of them and often lead exciting, productive lives.

Then there are other models who earn a good living doing what they love, work closely with designers, and get to try on some fabulous clothes, yet their faces aren't recognizable, they rarely travel, and they never walk a runway. They're "fit" models, employed by manufacturing companies or designers to be human mannequins on the which garments are fitted as samples are being created. While fit models used by high-fashion designers generally have the physical proportions that runway models have and are somewhere between a size two and four, some manufacturing companies require models that are a little bigger – often a size six or more – to fit clothes designed for larger women. Or if the company specializes in clothes for plus-size women or petite women, they choose their fit models accordingly.

While patience is key for any model who must stand on her feet at fittings, often for hours on end, the job of a fit model can be especially trying since garments are actually being designed, constructed, and "worked out" in those fit sessions. There's little perceived glamour that comes along with this job, as the location is mostly confined to design studios or the back rooms of factories where the clothes are made.

Specialty models come in all shapes and sizes. Generally, they are represented by special agencies, though some of the bigger agencies do have specific divisions that deal with those who are plus-size or petite.

Agent Ben Barry, who owns one of the foremost plus-size model agencies in Canada and who constantly works at broadening the ways the fashion industry sees beauty, says the demand for plus-size models has exploded. These models work primarily for commercial clients or specialty brands. Most range in dress size from twelve to eighteen, in age from sixteen to sixty plus, and in height from 5'8" to 5'11," and they come from all cultural backgrounds. As there hasn't been a great demand for them in the world of high fashion and opportunities for runway work were scarce until recently, some of these specialty models aren't up on runway technique. Barry says that plus-size models need to study and practice their catwalk. "But they cannot just take lessons from any fashion show featuring 'straight-size' models," explains Barry, "because the way a size-two model walks versus the way a size-fourteen model walks is different; they have different body types, so they move in their own unique way." Barry advises aspiring plus-size models to seek out those fashion shows featuring these plus models and replicate their walks, while adding their own confident techniques.

Crystal Renn's walk down the Chanel runway in Saint-Tropez marks the first plus-size model to walk for the label.

One of the top plus-size models working today is Florida-born Crystal Renn, who, at one point, boasted being a size fourteen. She began her career as a straight-size model, but developed an almost fatal eating disorder, living on a diet of lettuce, gum, and Diet Coke while trying to make it as a size zero. Realizing that changing her natural body shape was not only impossible but unhealthy, she went into recovery and returned to the fashion industry at her natural and healthy size. Since joining Ford Models Plus Division, the twenty-three-year-old has walked the runway for several impressive clients, including Jean Paul Gaultier and Chanel; appeared in print campaigns for Dolce & Gabbana and Mango; graced the covers of

Harper's Bazaar and *Elle Italia*; as well as appearing in *Vogue's* American, Italian, French, and German editions.

"What I love about plus-size modeling," says Crystal, "is that it takes all the pressure off of obsessing about numbers. I don't have to worry because I don't have to have thirty-four-inch hips. I can be exactly who I am, and I get to do the best job in the world." Truthfully, Crystal is likely no bigger than a size ten these days. But when you realize that most models are a size two or four, a size eight or ten is considered plus-size when it comes to average models.

Ben Barry stresses that just like straight-size models, plus models must work to maintain their appearance and stay healthy. They should exercise and eat well to maximize their energy, stamina, and physical form.

"How lucky am I to have a healthy body that allows me to do a job I love?" asks Liis Windischmann, a plus-size model who was discovered in a shopping mall and who has had a successful career for over fifteen years. "I feel blessed to be exactly who I am – mind, body, and soul – and be hired for it." Liis is especially grateful that she is a role model for self-confidence. "One of the highlights of my career," she reveals, "is that as a confident size-fourteen woman who has made it in a tough, competitive profession, I can pass on my stories of body confidence and perseverance to girls and teenagers in lectures and projects. I now speak in the media, encouraging increased self-esteem levels in society."

There are also models that are highly sought after because certain parts of their body – namely, their hands or feet – are especially beautiful. The work they do is generally confined to advertising: shooting campaigns for products like jewelry, nail polish, and hand cream. Despite the fact that their faces are rarely seen, these models are still paid well. Long slender hands, straight fingers, uniform nail beds, and smooth skin are some of the traits necessary for a hand model.

The exotic Shani Feldman has made "hand modeling" her specialty.

Model Shani Feldman has been a specialty hand model since she posed with a bottle of skin cream in Cape Town, South Africa, a few years ago. The resulting photo captured the beauty of her hands, and back in North America, her agent suggested she might want to do hand-modeling to supplement her income. "Basically, it takes nice hands," says Shani, "and an ability to move fluidly and slowly. Everything is ultra-precise when it comes to hand-modeling." But, whether for TV commercials or still photography, this type of modeling isn't anywhere near as satisfying as full-body modeling. "There's no real feeling when you're just using your hands," says Shani. "You just have to follow directions and be able to move your hands with great precision."

Some models are known as beauty models. Those who confine their work to beauty campaigns or magazine editorials have especially exquisite faces or luxurious manes of hair. And, because of that, they don't always have to meet the height requirements for runway modeling. But, realistically, so many models in the business today have "the complete package." And since most agencies are interested in signing girls that are versatile, someone who has just a remarkably gorgeous face and a great head of hair is unlikely to get the representation she'd need to get anywhere in this business.

Some commercial advertisers, like those that produce catalogs for retailers, often look for models that don't have a high-fashion look. So a girl who's not that tall, or who has more of a pretty girl-next-door look, has a much better chance

Julia Dunstall evidently knows how to work the accessories.

of getting work. These are not the kind of so-called "glamourous" jobs that involve travel or meeting international designers and photographers. Still, the work itself, while nowhere near as creative, artsy, or exciting as high fashion, can be quite lucrative, and for those who are still in school, can't really travel, and just want to make extra money in the business of posing, it makes sense. While these girls don't ever appear in fashion-magazine editorials, catalog models often get cast in TV commercials, and many are hired for local runway shows.

Another issue that's come up for models in the past few years is celebrities. Because we're living in a celebrity-obsessed society, which can't seem to get enough of those famous faces from TV and film, many design labels and cosmetics companies hire these stars to represent their brands and help sell their products. Celebrities also grace the covers of fashion magazines to a greater degree now than ever before. "Readers want to know more about celebrities' lives, their relationships, and their fashion sense," says *Flare* magazine's editor-in-chief, Lisa Tant. "At *Flare*, we mix our celebrity covers with top models that are well known in the fashion industry. But, in most cases, readers prefer celebrity covers," notes Tant. What it means is less lucrative work and less of that all-important exposure for models. And that's why, more and more, models are trying to cultivate other talents, like music, acting, or design. "I find girls like Coco Rocha – those who have a dancing, singing, or acting background – to be so much more vital than girls who model just because they have the looks," offers Tant.

While modeling is usually a short-lived career, lasting only until one's mid-twenties, some girls manage to work well beyond that, into their thirties. One model, Carmen Dell'Orefice, has starred in campaigns into her seventies! But that is an extremely rare case. Still, there are those supermodels that do go on to become iconic figures and such celebrities in their own rite that photographers are always thrilled to shoot them, magazines are happy to feature them, and designers will even use them to promote their brands. Icons like Linda Evangelista or Eva Herzigova are so revered in the business that they're even asked to make special guest appearances on some designers' runways. It's wonderful to see these "older" models still out there working and looking so beautiful. I often think how difficult it must be for them, surrounded by girls that are sometimes young enough to be their daughters.

As much as these older models are appreciated and celebrated, especially by older women, they come up against a lot of scrutiny. Despite all their experience and fame, they need an extreme amount of confidence to put themselves "out there," especially in an arena ruled by the young. It's a tough position to be in, and that's why the public and the media applaud these fabulous older models and are always excited to see them.

Ideally, designers design for "real" women – those who actually go into the shops, buy their creations, and wear them out into the world. But like all artistic beings, a designer's creative spark is fueled by inspiration. And in the fashion world, that inspiration is often found in a muse – a beautiful woman whose personality and inherent sense of style encourage the designer to dream and create. Sometimes, these muses are actresses.

Strutting it at the DSquared show, staged by Fashion Television, in Toronto.

In the 1950s and '60s, Audrey Hepburn was a powerful muse for the famous French designer Hubert de Givenchy. In the 1970s, American designers Halston and Bob Mackie gleaned a lot of inspiration from Liza Minnelli and Cher, respectively. The French actress Anna Mouglalis has been a great muse for Chanel's Karl Lagerfeld. And Marc Jacobs frequently looks to accomplished young women, like the director Sofia Coppola, for inspiration.

But designers are also greatly inspired by some of the outstanding models they work with. Quirky Irina Lazareanu has been a wonderful muse for Karl Lagerfeld in the past, as well as fueling the imagination of others designers, like Balenciaga's Nicholas Ghesquière. The great milliner Philip Treacy, whose outlandish hats never fail to get attention, has long been inspired by Irish-born model Erin O'Conner. Her strong, statuesque presence and strikingly dramatic profile, coupled with her keen intelligence and charming personality, have given Erin longevity in the business. It's obvious that her theatrical sensibility would inspire a hat designer like Treacy and make her the perfect model for his creations. And who can forget what the legendary Yves Saint Laurent did for black models when he embraced such exotic, dark-skinned beauties as the Somalian-born Iman.

The late Alexander McQueen never failed to stage inspiring spectacles.

IMAN

Birth date: July 25, 1955

Born in: Somalia

Agency: One Management (NYC), Independent Models (London)

Discovered: At the age of 19, by American photographer Peter Beard, who persuaded her to relocate to the United States

Big break/Career highlights:

- Known for being one of the first to challenge and change our notions of beauty
- Modeled for *Vogue* in 1976, inspiring Fashion Designer Yves Saint Laurent's African Queen couture collection. "My dream woman is Iman," he said.
- Appeared on television and in movies, including *Out of Africa*, *LA Story*, and *Heart of Darkness*
- Developed the cosmetics line IMAN for women of color
- Was shot by top photographers Steven Meisel, Helmut Newton, Richard Avedon, Irving Penn, and Annie Liebovitz

Career development: Was hit by a drunk driver while in a taxi in 1983, causing her face to be reconstructed; acted; hosted *Project Runway Canada*; became CEO of IMAN Cosmetics; was a spokesperson for the Keep a Child Alive program; married Musician David Bowie.

Often, a designer's "muse of the moment" (muses sometimes change from season to season) opens and/or closes the designer's runway show. That coveted role is a big honor for any model. Molly Sims – model, actress, and former MTV "House of Style" host – says she never had the honor of strutting that "first look," or first outfit, in a designer's show, but she recognizes that there's so much riding on that placing. "At the beginning of the show, it really starts the momentum, so you want someone like a Gisele (Bündchen), who can give you a dynamic opening, and everything just flows from there."

"Numero Uno is always the best!" enthuses Coca Rocha, who's often opened shows for designers. But Irina Lazareanu, a frequent muse, claims that as great as it is to open a Chanel or Dior show, the thrill can wear thin after a while. "When you do twenty shows in every city," she says, "you're like 'Whatever! Just tell me where to go, where to put my shoes on, and let me do my job because I have three shows after this!'"

NINE

STEPPING-STONE EXTRAORDINAIRE

One of the most exciting and magical things about life is that you never know where it's going to take you. Sure, we all have dreams about the future and schemes of how we *think* we're going to get from Step A to Step B. But life is filled with unexpected twists and turns.

I found myself in the fashion world by taking a very unconventional path – one I never dreamed would lead me here. While I always had an affinity for fashion, I aspired to be an actress (and began working professionally at the age of sixteen) and a mime artist. I studied my craft at university in Toronto and at performance schools in both New York and Paris. Then I moved to Newfoundland, where I wound up on the radio as a writer/broadcaster. After three years of honing my on-air skills, I returned to Toronto, where I landed another job in radio. Soon after, I was offered a job in television as a music reporter. I started reporting on the entertainment scene in general, but got excited when I heard that a TV show about fashion was being developed. The idea so intrigued me that I virtually talked my way into being host and segment producer of the show. And the rest is Fashion Television history.

As an aspiring teen actress, I never had an inkling that I'd wind up covering the international fashion scene for both television and print media. But, happily, I embraced each opportunity that came my way, worked extremely hard, and, eventually, learned a lot about the world and myself in the process.

Looking back, my journey into the fashion world seems like a natural, if unorthodox, progression. But I never saw it coming. It's important to have some sort of long-range goal in mind – even though that goal may change over time, morphing into something quite different. This rings especially true for those embarking on a career as traditionally short-lived as modeling. It can be sad indeed for a model to find herself suddenly no longer at the top of her game, with no real prospects.

Modeling is a performance art, and many girls, like Jessica Stam on the left, relish the chance to take part in the theatrics of a designer's creative, high-drama vision.

While some successful models do manage to juggle post-secondary-school studies with their careers for a while, most are forced to abandon their academics once all the work starts coming. If a model hasn't graduated because she has taken time off, she may decide to go back and complete her education. But life as an international model can be a fascinating education in itself, opening your mind to all kinds of possibilities. Usually, by the time a girl is ready to leave the spotlight, she has a pretty good idea of what other opportunities she wants to pursue. Sometimes, it's in an area that has little or nothing to do with fashion, but often, since fashion exposes models to a plethora of jobs within the industry, a girl will use her fashion experience to launch into a new career within the field.

There have been models, like the legendary Wilhelmina or Canada's Judy Welch or Sherrida Rawlings, who start their own modeling agencies. Other models develop such a great sense of style that they choose to become stylists or fashion editors, like 1970s model Tonne Goodman, who went on to become the fashion director of American *Vogue*. Some models draw on their runway expertise to become fashion-show producers and creative directors, like Toronto's Erika Larva of Monarch Events Group. She indicates that the time she spent modeling served as an "internship" for her current business. "I always knew I would have to find something else to do, something I would feel I was more in control of," shares Erika. "I wanted something that would provide me with a long-term career and steady income. I was always intrigued by show business, and so the transition to becoming a show producer seemed like the obvious choice," she explains.

Some models have a talent for teaching and capitalize on their catwalk experience by instructing other models how to strut it, like the inimitable Jamaican-born Stacey McKenzie, who runs Walk This Way Workshops. "When I started out, I had no guidance or support to help me along my journey getting into the modeling industry," explains Stacey. "I noticed that I wasn't alone and decided that, when the time was right, I would start a company to mentor model hopefuls, guiding them on the right path to help make it a little easier for them to make their dreams come true." Stacey says the thrill of watching her students evolve into confident human beings has been incredibly rewarding.

Some models become so intrigued with the process taking place on the other side of the lens that they go on to study the art of photography and become great photographers themselves. Take the famous Ellen von Unwerth – a German-born former model who's known for her strong ability to relax her subjects and shoot them in fun, unusual settings. "Being a former model, working with models is certainly easier," says Ellen. "They understand the images (I'm after) are about freedom and femininity. We're here to have fun." And Helena Christensen, the famous Danish supermodel, has also cultivated a career as a well-respected

JESSICA STAM

Birth date: April 23, 1986

Born in: Canada

Agency: IMG Models (NYC, London, Paris, Milan)

Discovered: At the age of 15, in a Tim Horton's coffee shop near Canada's Wonderland, by an agent from International Model Management in Barrie, Ontario

Big break/Career highlights:

- Won the Los Angeles Model Look Search in 2002
- Known for her casual cool walk on the runway and her ice blue-gray eyes
- Had her career jump-started by Photographer Steven Meisel, who cast her in every advertising campaign he was shooting
- Promoted her profile when Marc Jacobs created the Stam bag
- Earned an estimated $1.5 million in the year leading up to July 2007. Named the world's fifteenth highest-paid model, according to *Forbes* magazine
- Was the face of Bulgari, Lanvin, Christian Dior, Roberto Cavalli, Dolce & Gabbana, among others
- Dated Anthony Kiedis of the Red Hot Chili Peppers and DJ Adam Goldstein

Controversy: Sued for breach of contract in 2004 by New York Model Management

Career development: Hosted a charity event to build wells in Africa; worked on getting her pilot's license.

photographer. "I think it's so important that you have certain things in life that drive you, something that really means something to you, and photography means exactly that to me," she told me at one of her first exhibitions.

Because most models cultivate a great sense of personal style once they have a few seasons under their belt, many develop such a passion for the art of creation that they go on to become designers. Texan Erin Wasson ruled the runways for several years before she turned her talents to styling. After working as a stylist for the hot American designer Alexander Wang, she introduced her own jewelry line shortly thereafter. Then, for spring 2009, Erin collaborated with the surf and skate lifestyle brand RVCA, creating her own line for the company. "I've taken lots of pictures," says Erin, "but there is nothing like seeing the girls go down the runway in your designs. It's an emotion you can't explain," she tells me, "but it's a lot of work." Still, the satisfaction is worth it. "I've gotten to put my name on other people's products for so long, but now I get a chance to put my name on something I truly believe in, and I just feel so blessed."

Many others have successfully managed to launch collections, wisely capitalizing on all their connections and solid experience that modeling has given them. The Ukrainian-born American model, musician, and actress Milla Jovovich designed a wonderful clothing line with her friend, former model Carmen Hawk, from 2003 to 2008. The label was called Jovovich-Hawk. "I've never worked so hard to make something," Milla told me, shortly after they launched their first collection. "Designing a collection requires a lot of instinct and a lot of passion. It's hard work, but seeing your final piece is priceless," she said. "Now we care about something bigger than ourselves."

Christy Turlington, one of the original supermodels, has a penchant for yoga and has designed sports shoes and yogawear for Puma. The ever-stylish Kate Moss worked closely with Britain's Topshop to design a special collection bearing her name. Inès de la Fressange, a former model who once was a muse to Karl Lagerfeld, now heads up the legendary shoe design house of Roger Vivier in Paris. Another former model and muse to the late, great Yves Saint Laurent, Loulou de la Falaise, has her own clothing label and shop in Paris. Canada's Jessica Stam has collaborated on some pieces with the popular Rag &

PHOTO CREDIT: GETTY IMAGES

Bone label. And Somalian model Alek Wek started designing exquisite handbags a few years ago, under the label 1933. The list goes on.

Models who've become household names sometimes use their name brands to promote whole new businesses. Kathy Ireland, a famous American model from the 1980s, has created a number of highly successful fashion and home lines, producing everything from socks to chandeliers. She's also produced several workout videos and written a few books.

The gorgeous Australian model Elle Macpherson founded her own lingerie label as well as a

Australian supermodel Elle Macpherson is an astute and highly successful businesswoman who heads up her own lingerie label.

beauty products company. "I wanted to grow my own brand," she once told me. "I really thought to myself, 'Why am I promoting someone else's brand, when I have the opportunity to promote and manufacture my own products?'" Elle's also produced workout videos and is famous for the highly popular calendars she's created. And if that's not enough, she has acted in movies and was an executive producer on the short-lived TV series *The Beautiful Life*, based on the modeling world – a series in which she also starred.

America's iconic Cindy Crawford has her own successful line of furniture. Somalian-born legend Iman developed her own popular brand of makeup. Canada's Daria Werbowy fronted a small makeup line for L'Oréal. Eve Salvail, the former quirky Montreal native and one-time muse to Jean Paul Gaultier, tried her hand at being a financial advisor in New York and is now a successful international club deejay. British model Karen Elson has launched a musical career. These are only a few examples of the diverse occupations that a modeling career can lead to. Because modeling is a "business" and every model has to be business-savvy, it's no wonder that this world can be a great place to hone skills and make lots of personal and professional contacts. If a model keeps her eye on the prize and is determined to remain a success, even when her modeling days are over, there are endless possibilities of what she might dream up for herself for financial and creative fulfillment.

Some models aspire to expand their performance talents and become actresses or even broadcasters, like the amazing Tyra Banks. Talk about having the perfect combination of talent,

Tyra Banks celebrates Fashion Week with famed fashion-show producer Alexandre de Betak and model Alek Wek backstage.

ambition, brains, beauty, and tenacity! After getting her feet wet as a model and actor, she then formed her own production company, creating the wildly successful *America's Next Top Model* and her own daytime talk show. Other broadcasters that started out as models include British presenter Cat Deeley, host of the popular *So You Think You Can Dance*, and Canadian MuchMusic Veejay Sarah Taylor.

Many models know from the get-go that their work is only a stepping-stone to creative endeavors that are far more reaching and ultimately more satisfying. And some of the most famous and accomplished female actors ever wisely used their modeling careers as launching pads, including Halle Berry, Demi Moore, Angelina Jolie, Nicole Kidman, Natalie Portman, and Mischa Barton, to name a few.

One of the toughest challenges a model has to face when she wants to segue into acting is having to prove that she really is more than just a pretty face and that she possesses genuine talent. Generally speaking, only those who really demonstrate their commitment to growing artistically and who study the craft of acting will be taken seriously. Sometimes, it seems as though a model has to work twice as hard to earn credibility and respect as an actress. The cynics and the critics are usually out in full force. And, quite frankly, only the strong survive. Models who've attempted to make their mark as actresses, but who've been panned by critics include legends Naomi Campbell and Cindy Crawford. Nothing ventured, nothing gained, but risk-taking is crucial if you want to keep your career moving.

Few iconic models have managed to model well beyond what most in the industry can expect. But Canada's Linda Evangelista, one of the greatest models in fashion history who was discovered at the tender age of thirteen, is still nabbing major assignments today. In 2004, she told me that, unlike other models who desperately try to reinvent themselves, she's always been adamant about sticking to what she knows best. "Modeling has always been my primary focus," she explained. "Everyone was so worried about diversifying, so they went off and wrote books and made music and acted. And, I mean, what's wrong with staying a model? I think it's great to diversify, but it was my dream to model (since the age of twelve), and I'm still fulfilling my dreams every day that I get to work." It does require effort though. "I take such great care of myself. I learned to respect myself. I was so busy before, I had no idea how to do that."

Linda Evangelista's work continues to inspire all of us who love fashion. But she really is an exception to the rule: The majority of models abandon the scene well before the age of thirty. Sometimes, work simply dries up for them; other times, the pressures of modeling just become too much to handle.

The legendary Linda Evangelista first skyrocketed to international stardom in the 1990s, and her lucrative career continues to this day.

LINDA EVANGELISTA

Birth date: May 10, 1965
Born in: Canada
Agency: DNA Model Management (NYC), Models 1 (London)
Discovered: At the age of 13, by a talent agent at the 1978 Miss Teen Niagara contest
Big break/Career highlights:
- Credited with sparking the supermodel craze of the late 1980s and 1990s
- Called "the chameleon" for her frequently changing hair color and style and for her ability to transform in front of the camera
- Known for her often-misquoted statement "We don't wake up for less than $10,000 a day," spoken in 1990 to Jonathan Van Meter of *Vogue*

Career development: Was first married to Elite executive Gerald Marie; appeared in several music videos; was an advocate for AIDS and breast cancer research; became a Star on Canada's Walk of Fame; received the 1996 VH1 Fashion Awards Lifetime Achievement Award.

And there are many sad stories about talented models that simply "fall through the cracks," becoming victims of drug abuse or eating disorders because they try so hard to please that they lose sight of themselves.

The best advice for those who aspire to a career in modeling is to live in the present; take ultra-good care of yourself, both physically and emotionally; savor each and every wonderful experience that comes your way, but keep one eye firmly focused on the future. The older you get, the more you'll realize that the world is an awfully big place, with countless exciting possibilities that you may have never even imagined. You can be the master of your own destiny if you keep your nose to the grindstone, take advantage of opportunities, and hold fast to your dreams.

A MODEL EDUCATION

Embarking on a modeling career doesn't necessarily mean abandoning your formal education. Many models still manage to complete university or college degrees while handling various modeling assignments. It may not be easy, but for those with the right passion and discipline, it's astounding what can be accomplished. And while some girls that attend high school may be able to restrict their modeling to school holiday breaks, various programs run through secondary schools are especially geared for those students with intense, extracurricular involvement. Besides young models, these programs cater to actors, dancers, musicians, and athletes. Toronto's Kate Somers attended one such program and speaks very positively of her experience, which required a lot of work online. "The setup is perfect for high-school students balancing careers and extracurricular activities who still wish to excel in their studies," she says. Kate would never consider dropping her schoolwork in order to take it up once her modeling work wanes. "This industry can be extraordinarily temporary," she says, "and an education is the only pillar of support to fall back on. A career in high fashion can bring adventure, travel, and knowledge in many forms, but it can't bring a degree in law or medicine. My family and my agents have always stressed the importance of finishing school so that my potential can be realized in more ways than one."

DARIA WERBOWY

Birth date: November 19, 1983

Born in: Poland (immigrated to Toronto at the age of 3)

Agency: IMG Models (NYC)

Discovered: At the age of 14, in a national modeling contest

Big break/Career highlights:

- After little success, followed Elite scout Elmer Olsen as he opened his own agency
- Became the face for Prada, photographed by Steven Meisel
- Holds the record for opening and closing the most shows in one season
- Has appeared on the covers of *W*, *V*, *Vogue*, Italian *Vogue*, French *Vogue*, British *Vogue*, and Japanese *Vogue*
- Her 2004 American *Vogue* shoot with iconic photographer Helmut Newton was his last before his death in a car accident
- Listed in the top ten highest-earning models in the world for the last four years

Career development: Became the face and spokesperson for Lancôme; was the face for Hermès for Fall 2007; became the face for Dior for Fall 2008; was the face for Roberto Cavalli for Fall 2009; joined Canada's Walk of Fame in 2008, the award presented to her by Jeanne Beker.

Supermodel Daria Werbowy, seen here with Karl Lagerfeld, is one of the world's most photographed models.

While no one can emphasize enough the value of getting a formal education, there's something to be said about what you can learn about life via the modeling world. With all the discipline required, mandatory travel, and wide assortment of people you get to meet, most seasoned models say the nature of the business, and the lifestyle it dictates, are real eye-openers. "Modeling gave me an education I don't think school could have provided me with – like meeting Karl Lagerfeld, for instance, and working as closely with him as I did, listening to him and the inspirations. I don't think I could have gotten that at any school, ever," says top American model Carolyn Murphy.

GISELE BÜNDCHEN

Birth date: July 20, 1980

Born in: Brazil

Agency: IMG Models (NYC), 2pm Model Management (Copenhagen)

Discovered: At the age of 14, by an agent eating at a McDonald's restaurant in São Paulo

Big break/Career highlights:

- Placed second in the Elite Look of the Year contest
- Arrived on the scene at the end of the "heroin chic" era
- Appeared on the June 1999 cover of *Vogue* with the headline "The Return of the Sexy Model"
- Graced three consecutive *Vogue* covers – November 1999, December 1999, and January 2000
- Named "the most beautiful girl in the world" in 2000 by music magazine *Rolling Stone*
- Appeared on over 500 magazine covers, including *W*, *Harper's Bazaar*, *Elle*, *Allure*, and the international editions of *Vogue*
- Named the highest-paid model in the world since 2001, with an estimated $150 million fortune, according to *Forbes* magazine
- Did campaigns for all the top design houses, including Christian Dior, Balenciaga, Dolce & Gabbana, Versace, Givenchy, Lanvin, Valentino, Ralph Lauren, Michael Kors, and Louis Vuitton
- Had a multi-million-dollar deal with Apple Inc.

Brazilian bombshell Gisele Bündchen's playful approach to fashion makes her easy to work with and keeps her philosophical about what matters in life.

Controversy: During a Victoria's Secret show, Gisele was the target of People for the Ethical Treatment of Animals (PETA), when members jumped onstage holding signs that read "Gisele: Fur Scum." She said the protest was unwarranted as she loves animals and does not wear fur.

Career development: Acts as a goodwill ambassador for the United Nations Environment Program; lends her support and image to a number of charities and humanitarian causes; developed her own line of sandals called Ipanema Gisele Bündchen. Naomi Campbell said, "Kate Moss is obviously a supermodel, but after Gisele, I don't think there's been one."

For Angela Lindvall, the educational value of her modeling experience was all about the people. "The biggest thing I've learned," she says, "is to accept and appreciate different kinds of people. You're around so many people from so many places. Maybe you wouldn't hang out with these characters in your everyday life. But you accept them for who they are."

Ethiopian-born model Liya Kebede also spells it out. "In the fashion industry, you see people from all walks of life. You deal with all sorts of problems. So it really is like a school of life, in a way," she says.

Britain's Stella Tennant claims one of the most interesting things she's learned is seeing what happens to people when they become successful. "I've seen what money can do to people, what power can do . . . what fame does . . . ," she says. "Some manage it very well, and others fall by the wayside."

The supreme success experienced by Gisele Bündchen has served her well. The Brazilian supermodel says that modeling taught her to be independent and to deal with things in a much more serious way. "It taught me to take responsibility for things. Being so young and having to answer for your actions is a little strange.

PHOTO CREDIT: CTV

Normally, when you're fourteen or fifteen, you don't really have to do that. But when you're in this business, you do have to," she explains. "You grow up faster . . . mature faster."

Naomi Campbell says the biggest lesson she's learned from modeling has to do with taking responsibility for your own happiness. "No one

At Dior's 60th anniversary celebration at Versailles, with the inimitable Naomi Campbell.

else can do that for you," she reflects. "I think it's just maturity. I've been living half my life in front of the cameras, the press, the world. There's no book that teaches you how to act and how to be and how to deal with this life we're living. You just have to learn from your mistakes, pick yourself up, dust yourself off, and keep going." Naomi adds that the industry has also taught her a lot about giving back — to use what you've become to help others.

Czech supermodel Karolina Kurkova, one of the industry's top earners, says that remembering your roots is what it's all about. "I think it's always important to remember where you're from," she says. "Remember your parents, your background, and really appreciate everything you have." Karolina is also philosophical about the "easy come, easy go" nature of success in this business. "One day you get it, one day you lose it," she notes.

Britain's Agyness Deyn echoes these sentiments. "You've got to remember where you came from and what you were doing before you were a model," she says. "I'm from Manchester, and I was a normal kid: I went to school, I had jobs. . . . You have to really appreciate the chance you've been given."

And veteran model Kristen McMenamy, who made her mark in the late 1980s and '90s with her androgynous look and quirky style and who recently resurfaced on a couple of Paris runways, claims that, while the business has changed a lot in the last twenty years, "It's still the best job in the world, *if* you can keep your head on your shoulders."

Agyness Deyn camps it up.

Daria Werbowy makes it a priority to keep her head out of the clouds. "I definitely force myself to stay grounded and do things that will keep me that way," she says. She also surrounds herself with people who help ground her. "I just think life's too short to get lost in the shuffle and lose yourself along the way," she muses. To keep her feet firmly planted in reality, she spends a lot of time with her closely knit family. "I also love being around nature," Daria says, "so I snowboard and sail a lot. I also love cooking and taking care of my cats . . . really kind of normal stuff. At the end of the day, I like the simple life." But Daria is also concerned with challenging herself in new ways, now that she has such success as a model under her belt. "I'm really interested in pushing myself from a spiritual perspective," she tells me, "and discovering why I'm here on this planet and what my duty is to myself and to the people around me. That's definitely something you start to think about as you get a little older."

Some of the best advice comes from Yasmin Warsame, who urges aspiring models to be self-aware and to always stay true to themselves. "Just be yourself, and you can't go wrong," she suggests. "As long as you can go to your bed and sleep at peace, that's what matters. And make sure whatever you're doing serves a purpose within you, that you're happy with it, that you feel you're really meant to do it . . . it's all about your inner self."

Somalian-born model Yasmin Warsame has cultivated a career with longevity. Her stellar exotic look and deep sensitivity have set her apart.

The fashion world can be a pretty fabulous place: exciting, creative, entertaining, and productive. But, with its overblown egos, high drama, and fickle nature, it can also be a place that makes you crazy. It is not for the fainthearted. I often regard the fashion arena as a microcosm for life and have learned countless invaluable lessons about human nature in its trenches. Unquestionably, it can provide a vibrant and stimulating backdrop for a girl to grow up in, but that girl must have her head screwed on right if she's going to not only survive in that world, but really thrive. Remaining realistic is imperative: The media has glamourized and glorified the model's role in fashion, but this coveted "role" is physically and psychologically demanding. As with life, there's an awful lot of grit behind that glamour. I've learned that you simply can't have one without the other.

JEANNE BEKER
AT SIXTEEN

ACKNOWLEDGMENTS

As host of Fashion Television over the past twenty-five years, I've learned a lot about what makes the fashion world go round and what it takes to not only climb up onto this wondrous carousel, but how to stay on the ride. One thing that's become obvious to me is that the more accomplished someone is, the easier they make it all look. I'm forever grateful to my Fashion Television family – especially Jay Levine and Howard Brull – for consistently producing the kind of television that's both edifying and entertaining. A giant thank-you goes to the incredible Christopher Sherman, for always being there for me in so many ways and for helping with the research for this book; to the sage and savvy Sue Tate, editor extraordinaire, whose own experiences with her "model daughter" gave me an invaluable point of view; to Elmer Olsen, superstar scout and agent, for being so darn good at what he does; and to *Top Model*'s inimitable Jay Manuel, who opened my eyes to tough love when it came to dealing with those girls with stars in their eyes.

Also, many thanks to the talented FQ art teams I had the honor of working with over the years – first, Ric Little and Asha Hodura, and later, Bob Makinson and Abel Munoz – who brought so many great models to the pages of our magazines; and to all those brilliant photographers who captured the magic. Of course, it's the girls themselves who inspire us all with their passion, personality, and perseverance. A big hug to those I've had the pleasure of meeting over the years, as we all strutted through fashion's trenches: It's been a privilege to watch you grow. Big kisses to all my dear friends, my fabulous sister, Marilyn, and my steadfast Bear. And, finally, heartfelt thanks to my gorgeous mom, Bronia, and my two amazing daughters, Bekky and Joey, who constantly remind me of beauty's true nature.